Memoirs of a BABYBOOMER

Memoirs of a
BABYBOOMER

Growing up in Charleston, South Carolina
BY RUDOLPH F. WIGGINS
AKA RUDOLPH FRAZIER
MARY [sic] SON

To order additional copies of this book, contact:
Xlibris Corporation
1-888-795-4274
www.Xlibris.com
Orders@Xlibris.com
118620

FOREWORD

IT HAS BEEN a life-long ambition of the author to chronicle his years growing up in the historic city of Charleston, South Carolina amid such momentous events as the proliferation of television sets in America's households, horse-drawn carts, integration, the moon landing, segregation, the Psychedelic Movement, the Funkedelic Movement, etc. Because the author pretty much led a sheltered life while growing up, his ability to speak from a personal experience on all these topics will be limited somewhat but he will touch on those aspects that he **was** able to relate to on a personal basis and in the process, give you some insight into life, as it were, in one of the south's most genteel towns during that period.

CHAPTER 1

IN OR ABOUT the year 2004, I set out to publish this book. The first draft made prior to 2004 went like this: "As I approach the half century mark, I find . . . ." Well, I was forty-eight when I wrote the first draft. Five years later and having arrived at fifty-three, I've finally decided to finalize my book. It's about memoirs of American ideals, customs and values that I experienced growing up in one of the country's premier southern towns—Charleston, South Carolina—and my overall view and opinionated comments regarding them. I'd like the reader to come with me now, particularly the 'baby boomer' as we are called and reminisce about the Americana that was.

I was born in the mid-fifties in a small rural town in South Carolina called Ridgeland. At the age of one or so, my parents migrated to Charleston, South Carolina. Charleston or Charles Towne as it was originally called, having been named after King Charles II of England, is the second largest city in South Carolina after Columbia. My first memory of life in the streets of Charleston was walking along a street with my mother and seeing a horse (with blinders) for the first time hitched up to a cart and hearing the loud sounds of the hooves hitting the pavement as it went along. On the cart was a great big block of ice. "Ice man, ice man!" went the cry. I also recall horse-drawn carts carrying vegetables and the vendor crying out, "Ve-ge-tub-ble man, ve-ge-tub-ble man!" his thick, geechee South Carolinian accent allowing. In retrospect, I find it amusing now because prior to entering school and learning the proper pronunciation for the word, 'vegetable,' I found myself mimicking the vendors at that time. I'd often say, "Moma, the ve-ge-tub-ble man is outside." One of the other earlier experiences that stuck in my mind was an experience I had while walking with my mother down Hanover Street one day. I must have been, I'd say 3 or 4, walking beside my mother with her holding my hands, when I stopped suddenly—frozen in my tracks at the sight of a hobbling woman approaching us with two 'wooden supports' under each arm and a 'long white thing' on one of her legs. It was my first sight of someone with a cast on a broken leg (with crutches). For you Generation 'X-ers,' a cast is a plaster of Paris casing once used to support a broken bone. I say 'once used' because I can't recall seeing a cast within the last ten years. Anyway, I remember stopping and crying hysterically as the woman approached. My mother finally had to pick me up and carry me. As the woman passed, she said, partly to assuage my mother, "Yes, pick 'em up. He don't know wha' dis is!" pointing to the cast on her leg.

My first song recollected was that of Toni Fischer, *The Big Hurt*. My sister and I, if I remember correctly, were being babysitted by a friend of my mother's on America Street (the projects) and I recall running playfully around the grounds while hearing the song either being played or coming from a radio in a window.

My father, who I vaguely remember, having passed away when I was only ten, was a cook for the county jailhouse. I do remember him giving my sister and I a fierce beating after finding us fighting. I remember him often lying in bed and letting my sister and I play in his long hair (combing, brushing, and parting), taking us out on walks, making the rounds on Columbus Street and . . . . showing us off to his friends. On one of those outings, I heard Nat King Coles' *Ramblin' Rose* coming from a window of one of the houses we passed.

The state of South Carolina is steeped in mysticism and strange customs when it comes to folk magic and alternative medicines. I mention this because at about the age of ten or so, I became ill and subsequently confined to my bed for some time. When I got well enough to go back to school, my mother had me wear an asafetida bag. For those of you who do not know what an asafetida bag is, and I suspect there are many, it is a small bag (worn around the neck underneath the clothing) containing the roots of plants. It has a very distinctive smell to it and its purpose is to ward off sickness.

As a young boy living on Chapel Street, I led a solitary life, reading a lot of comic books. Because I was becoming ill more frequently as time went by, the family doctor suggested we move from the house on Chapel Street. My mother took the advice and we soon moved into the first three-story house(facing the cemetery) on Elizabeth Street. Shortly after, my mother's older sister and her five kids moved in with us. This was a life-changing event for me, my brothers and sister. There was my mother and her four kids, the sister next to her with her five kids and the younger of the three sisters. We all co-existed as one big family.

As young kids we were typical, you might say. We played lots of softball in our big backyard. When we didn't have a ball, we used the heads of dolls and all the neighbors' windows were fair game when we played. The inevitable scenario that took place when we played ball was that somebody would hit the ball (or dollhead) out of the yard into a neighbor's window, everyone would immediately put their hands to their ears, muffling out the sound of the neighbor's holler at having a ball come crashing through their window. We would then run under the house, to the corner or anywhere but stay at the scene of the crime.

I would like to say a little more about the small town where I spent my early years—Charleston, South Carolina. Charleston proper—forty years ago was a segregated town with whites south of Calhoun Street and blacks north of Calhoun. This arrangement was more a matter of lineage and to some extent economics rather than racism, I suppose, as a great number of the antebellum homes south of Calhoun street were passed down from wealthy plantation owners to present day descendants who were naturally white.

If a newcomer to our shores wanted to see a glimpse of the small, all-American town, he or she has only to visit Charleston, South Carolina. There, they will find quaint shops, warm, down-to-earth people and a plethora of historic landmarks. During the fifties and early sixties there were the small five-and-dime stores like McCory's, Woolworth, Kress and Edward's. Then there were the . . . . Well, just visit your local library and . . . . Oops! I was about to say—Visit your local library and look the artist Norman Rockwell up and you will have seen the Charleston of yesteryear, but this is two thousand eleven and you're more likely to place his name in the web browser of your computer or smart phone. Having been born at a time that I would like to think was a special time in American history, I feel fortunate to have witnessed the Civil Rights Era and barring the obvious problems the country faced at the time, a simpler and kinder America. I'm sure if you were to talk to various people born in different eras of America's history, each one of those people, I'd wager, would think they were born at a very special time in history but I think true historians will agree with me when I say the period between the latter fifties into the seventies was one of the most tumultuous periods in American history barring perhaps the Civil War era. Of course, I wasn't around during the Roaring Twenties or the Depression Years. Nonetheless, I'm going to stick with my original claim.

CHAPTER 2

WATCHING TELEVISION DURING the late fifties and early sixties was a novel pastime for many Americans. I remember the great jingles that permeated the television industry back then. Hey, babyboomers, do you remember these jingles—"Winston taste good, like a um, um cigarette should!" "Plop, plop, fizz, fizz, o' what a relief it is . . . . ," "Mr. Clean, Mr. Clean . . . . !" And then there were the shows—77 Sunset Strip, Gunsmoke, the Untouchables, Route 66, Rawhide, the Honeymooners, Happy Raine. Happy Raine? Yes, Happy Raine! Unless you grew up in Charleston, I wouldn't expect readers to know about this native American(woman) characterization who came on every weekday evening at 5:00p.m. The participants of the show were children of my age at the time. I'd say the age group was 5 to 8 years of age. In addition to interviews by the host, Happy Raine, there were games and Hanna Barbara cartoons, e.g. Deputy

Dog, Yogi Bear, and Quick Draw Mc Graw. A great deal of my sense of security was derived from this show because it was usually about this time in the evening that my mother would be in the kitchen preparing dinner for the evening and I guess I, unconsciously, associated the two. Later on in life I would wonder whether I enjoyed Happy Raine so much because I had associated it with my mother's good cooking or whether I had enjoyed my mother's cooking so much because I associated it with my favorite evening program, Happy Raine. I think the reason those early shows on television had such a psychological and emotional imprint was because it was a time of innocence for both me and the nation. I had no concerns at that time as my mother and father took care of all that. As the author sees it, people tend to perceive and interpret what they see according to their filtering process (their minds). A young child, having minimal prior experience to clog this filtering process might be able to perceive things in an unadulterated fashion. Additionally, the fifties saw a proliferation of television sets in American households and with it, a host of wholesome, clean shows, e.g. Ozzie and Harriet, The Donna Reed Show, My Three Sons, etc. Recently, I watched one or two of the shows I watched as a child and sure enough it was not the same. There was *something* missing! Could that *something* have been my innocence?

I want to inject this anecdote here that took place in the 70's. If it seems out of place, that's because it is, being inserted here this year 2012. I am putting it in as it is a late revision which includes a vivid memory of my mother and one of America's most zanniest comediennes. We were living on Jackson Street and I came home early one morning. My mother was sitting on the living room sofa going through her mail and watching I Love Lucy. As I watched her watching Lucy in one of her wild escapades, she suddenly says, "That Lucy too fool!"

Let's go now to 1960. Milkmen are making morning deliveries to homes all across the country, service station attendants are wearing uniforms, hats, bow ties and not only clean windows but ask customers if they would like to have their oil checked. The suburban moms' car of choice, during this time, is a wooden-paneled Ford station wagon. A few years later, I'm in elementary or grade school and every morning before class activities begin, we face the flag with our right hand over our chest and mouth the words—"I pledge allegiance to the flag of the United States Of America and to the Republic for which it stands, one nation under God, indivisible and liberty for all."

Now, during the writing of my first draft, as I wrote this very sentence, the day's date was June 26th,2002. It had been weeks between the last paragraph and this paragraph. As so often was the case, I had a tendency to write in spurts depending on the motivation. Incredibly and ironically, between the lapse of time, a furor erupted over the Pledge of Allegiance. The courts were saying that the Pledge was unconstitutional because of the phrase, "under God." Only time will tell if the Pledge will remain intact with no deletions or alterations.

Before I go on to the mid-sixties and later, I'd like to touch on the state of security at the schools during this time. In all honesty, I must admit that I do not know what, if any, security existed at the various schools in and around the country during this era. I can only speak for the schools in my town. What I remember is that there was very little security, as we know it today. In fact, all gates and entrances to schools were not only kept open during school hours but were routinely unmanned. If you wanted to visit a school, you'd simply walk right in using one of the many entrances. To the schools' credit though, all visitors were required to go to the offices and get a 'pass' as a formality upon entering the buildings. Again, let me reiterate that security was practically non-existent during these times which is not to say that there wasn't a need for it but rather administrators were not so much ensconced in the idea of security as they are now. As for violence or aberrant behavior—in retrospect— I'd *like* to say that there was no violence at the various schools in my town to perpetuate the idea that everything was just hunky dory back then. The truth be told, human nature has been the same since the advent of man and it was no different back in the 60's though on a smaller scale depending on what side of the tracks you lived. Sadly, I must admit *there* was violence though not on the horrendous scale we find it in some of our schools today. In all my school years, I can honestly say that I did not experience any serious problems having attended Columbus Street, Courtenay Elementary Schools and subsequently going on to Rivers High and ultimately Charleston High. My mother, God bless her, knew that I could never survive at our local high schools, so I was enrolled into Rivers high, a racially-mixed school across town, upon leaving grade school.

My memory of Rivers High was having to walk through a parking lot situated adjacent to the school every morning. Before I go any further along this line of thought, I'd like to tell readers that today is January 3rd, 2007 and the nation is in the aftermath of the death of two of the people I mention in my book here—Mr. James Brown and former President Gerald R. Ford. I mention the two men in that order because Mr. Brown left us first on Christmas day of 2006 and our former President, a day later. Our former President, in his nineties, had been out of the public's eye for quite some time and though there was some talk about him being gravely ill just prior to his death, his passing was surprising news. James Brown, a performer of the first magnitude, a legend and American icon whose dance moves were imitated by scores of artists, had become the personification of an era—sic transit gloria mundi. Now, getting back to that parking lot. The lot was the location of a venue called County Hall and Charleston's smaller version of the Apollo Theater here in New York. County Hall was was not only a place for special events but a place where entertainers and notable speakers made their appearances. All the entertainment stars who were anybody would appear there and I can remember many mornings walking through the lot and looking up at the marquee and seeing big name stars. One name that stuck in my mind was the name of *James Brown and his Famous Flames* and on one rare occasion I saw on the marquee:

Rev. Martin Luther King
Appearing Here Tonite

I say 'rare' because I enrolled at Rivers High in September of '67 and Dr. King had left us by April, the following year.

I want to go back now, and I'll be rewinding and forwarding during this read, so please bear with me. I had an amusing experience in the late 50's or very early 60's. At the time though, I was so young, I didn't know how to react. My mother's younger sister, being my youngest aunt, was staying with us during this time and would prove to be in the years to come a big influence in bringing all the energy and vitality of a teenager to our home. Anyway, she took me to the Lincoln theater one evening to see my first movie, *Reptilicus*, a sci-fi thriller about a pre-historic dinosaur coming to life in modern times. I remember sitting there, watching the coming attractions. One coming attraction had a white woman lying on a gurney delivering a baby. Here's the shocker. The doctor pulls the baby out of the woman and it is ***BLACK?!*** As the doctor holds this black baby up in dramatic fashion by an ankle (above the mother), across the screen goes this horrific writing. The type you would see in a Vincent Price or Boris Karloff thriller. I remember the look of shock on the woman and doctor's face. Years later, I would think to myself, the doctor may have been genuinely shocked but why was the woman so shocked (laughing)!

Another memorable and amusing story I had related to me by . . . . It was about this time, the 50's, that the cleaning product, Mr. Clean, was being introduced to the public. Door-to-door salespeople were making their rounds in communities all across the city of Charleston with 13oz. bottles of Mr. Clean samples. Unfortunately, it seems their desire to get the product out before the public superceded plans for assigning specific salespeople to specific locales which ultimately resulted in salespeople crisscrossing into each other's territory. That being said, a salesman visited a home one day with his free sample for the occupant and proceeded to sell a young woman there on the new product. The woman, with her little boy nearby, affected her best demure, naïve impression and even made, what we call today, FAQs (**F**requently **A**sked **Q**uestions). Having satisfied himself that he had sold the woman on the new product, the salesman gave her the free sample and proceeded down the stairs, smiling confidently. The little boy who had been listening intently and quietly, suddenly said, "Oh boy, now we got **two**!" You could have bowled that salesman over with a feather! I would imagine that that salesman had quite a story to tell his colleagues back at the office that evening. Speaking of salesmen, my mother established a platonic friendship with a door-to-door salesman in the early sixties with the name, 'Mr. DooGood!' He was a big burly black man who carried a big trunk fill of lotions, soaps, oils, salves, etc. Whenever he would call on us and I'd answer the door, he would say, "Boy, way ya' momma at?" I'd go running into the house and I'd say, upon finding my mother, "Momma, Mr. DooGood is outside!" Many years later I wondered about that name. Was that really his name or just a name he concocted to offset the image of being a 'snake oil salesman.'

Ah yes, the 60's! For me the 60's was particularly memorable in that it was my first full decade, having been born in 1954. I emphasize this because as I iterated previously we have a tendency to respond to life based on our prior experiences (negative or positive), so having hardly any prior experiences and no negative experiences of consequence, my perception of the 60's was unadulterated and awe-inspiring. Growing up in Charleston, I can remember . . . . Oops! Here I go again—showing my age and sounding like those adults I would hear talking about the past when I was a kid. Anyway, I remember passing by this great, big ominous-looking house on my way to grade school every morning on Elizabeth Street in the early sixties. The stone walls surrounding the house were at least nine feet high and the ironworks on the gates appeared to be miniature skull heads. The house had fallen into disrepair and did lend some credence to the belief among the kids that it was haunted or worse—that a witch lived there. It wouldn't be until some twenty years or more after leaving home and returning to visit that I would discover that that dreaded house, having been declared a historical landmark, was the Aiken-Rhett House, the residence of a former governor of South Carolina! That 'witch' that occupied the house in the 60's turned out to be a . . . . ! I have avoided completing the last thought as to do so might be interpreted by South Carolinians as somewhat defaming. Suffice to say, the "witch" was just a figment of young minds having ran amuck. Getting back to the house, it had also been a rest stop for Jefferson Davis, the President of the Confederacy during the Civil War, before visiting the Battery where the first shot of the Civil War was fired. If the reader would like to know more about the historic city of Charleston, the author suggest you visit the web. I went online recently, contemplating downloading photos or illustrations for my book here—particularly a photo of the illustrious Aiken-Rhett House. I was prepared to do it until I discovered that the present day house, having undergone the preservation process, had lost some of its character. Before I go any further, I'd like to commend the Preservation Society on the splendid job they did in restoring the house to its former self. Absolutely marvelous. Looking at current photos of the house though, I promptly decided not to use them and instead, give my readers the opportunity to use their imagination toward what little description I have conveyed here (about the house) in helping them conjure up the image of the decrepit, ghostly mansion of the early 60's. To give you some idea of how much life had changed from the 1860's (the era of the Civil War and slavery) to the 1960's—African Americans populated all of Charleston proper including the immediate area surrounding the former Governor's mansion on Elizabeth Street. My family, which consisted of my mother, her four kids, her older sister and five kids, and my mother's youngest sister and brother all stayed within a few blocks south of the mansion on Elizabeth Street. We stayed in the first white house (on Elizabeth Street) adjacent to Chapel Street facing the cemetery. I remember the neighborhood being black and family-oriented. Additionally, the city had builted a black school

(Courtenay Elementary), a recreational facility and one or two night spots to accommodate the burgeoning population. In my mind, I've often tried to visualize life in this area during the 1860's:

[As I stand on the Mary Street wing of the Aiken-Rhett House, where before there were all black faces, the sounds of car engines and laughter emanating from lively children playing, I now hear the sound of hooves hitting the ground and aside from black servants, all the residents I see milling about are well-dressed white men, some of Charleston's, if not the south's, elitest coterie of citizens. As I stand there in front of the house, suddenly my attention is drawn to the opening garage door. As the door opens, out comes a contingent of about six horses hitched to a carriage and manned by a black footman.

They turn east on Mary Street heading for East Bay. There seems to be a sense of urgency. I now turn my attention toward the front of the house. I turn onto Elizabeth Street heading toward Wragg Square. As I walk along the street, I hear the distant sound of cannon blasts. As I come around on Wragg Square, I see between twenty and thirty men gathered in front of the house. Some having, what appears to be, newspapers. Some not. The discussion among the men seems to be very animated. As I turn and re-focus my eyes on the area to assess the overall atmosphere, I see ten to fifteen smaller groups of men springled over the square.]

CHAPTER 3

ONE DAY BACK on November 22, 1963, I remember my
principal walking into the classroom and, in a fit of emotion,
shouting to our teacher, "They've shot the President!" I don't remember
much else, except that the class was let out early.

In 1965, I'm in the fifth grade and school has just been let out
and I and all the other boys like myself are running home to watch
Batman and Robin. For you Generation X-ers, that was Burt Ward and
the inimitable Adam West who in the lexicon of that time, was rapidly
becoming a 'cool cat' and a personification of the 60's. About a year,
later we would see Van Williams and Bruce Lee as the Green Hornet
duo and witness our first Japanese sci-fi thriller, Ultra Man.

My younger aunt, who was staying with us in the 60's, was mostly
responsible for my introduction to 45rpm's and all the sounds of the
60's. I can vividly recall waking up school mornings to the sounds

of the Four Tops or Diana Ross and the Supremes. It was through my aunt I saw all the latest dance crazes, e.g. 'the funky chicken', 'the twist', 'the duck', 'the bird',etc. Music was such an integral part of the 60's until I find it unimaginable that *it* and 'the 60's' could have existed without the other. Growing up as a teenager in my own cultural sphere, I was introduced to people like Aretha Franklin, The Temptations, Mary Wells, The Supremes, James Brown, etc. etc. but across the bridge, kids were getting to know people or groups like Creedence Clearwater Revival, Jefferson Airplane, The Beatles, The Beach Boys, Janis Joplin, Santana, etc. etc. I suppose we all have idols during our teen years and I was no different and there were many artists—black and white—of all genres, American and British. I want to remind my readers politely that this is *my* frank account of what has been commonly referred to as the 'baby boomer' years and how **I** interpreted them. Along with my interpretation, I have also given my opinion regarding various topics or subjects. This having been said, I'd like to say now that as a teenager, I was never a fan of The Beatles or Elvis Presley. Being African-American this would appear to be a no-brainer to both my lighter and darker complexioned readers but . . . . The author believes that many times personalities are chosen either by peers or slick marketers (oftentimes called promoters) and thrust upon us (the public) and we in our gullibility are expected to . . . . But don't get me wrong, I think Elvis and The Beatles were charismatic entities, I just never became a part of the mass hysteria that involved these two entities. I thought about it long and hard as to why I was not affected by the hysteria surrounding two of the biggest pop entities of the baby boomer era and concluded that being African American had nothing to do with it but rather other factors.

After all, I did like James Taylor, the Beach Boys, the Carpenters, the Freshmens, the Righteous Brothers, ecetera, ecetera.

Having been born in the state of South Carolina was to be born into a state of conservatism and being raised in Charleston, a city noted for its numerous churches and synagogues, were strong confirmations of the state's conservative bent. Additionally, Charleston might be looked upon as the archetype of southern gentility and, if I'm not mistaken, was voted to be the most well-mannered city in the U.S. back in the '90s. Given these factors along with my conservative upbringing from a mother who never drank, smoked or swore and the fact that I attended schools with educators and fellow students who served to further enhance the whole concept of conservatism, I might think that all these things would be good reasons for my indifference toward "The King" and the Beatles. But please don't be misled into thinking that I was a model of conservatism because I, like millions of teenagers past and present, was instinctively feeling more and more rebellious as I matured but there was just some aspect of my make-up, whether it was instinctive or . . . , that prevented me from embracing . . . .

I'd like my readers to know that this is my third draft here and that earlier drafts spelled out in clear and specific terms exactly why I did not embrace Mr. Presley. By the time I had gotten to my third and final draft, I had decided that the legacy and memory of Elvis should be preserved, if only to assuage the millions of Elvis fans. Since the architect or architects of the Elvis phenomena had so succeeded in inculcating the masses, it would be futile to even . . . . . Additionally, I had begun to feel that voicing my opinion as I had about the country's biggest pop idol would have a 'tainting effect' on my memoirs and I did promise myself at the outset that I would keep my memoirs positive and not take my readers into the abyss. And so out of respect for our *dearly departed*, the millions of Elvis fans, and the former prime minister of Japan—Mr. Junichiro Koizumi—who I understand is a big Elvis fan, my final word(s) on Elvis will be—Elvis was a great American who contributed mightily to the pop culture of America. As for the Beatles, as unbelievable as it may sound, I saw nothing in their persons or their music that led me to think they were special. My affinities lied with lesser known British artists such as Gerry and the Pacemakers, the Animals, Petula Clark, Lulu, etc. By the way babyboomers, don't you think Lulu managed to capture the feel and mood of the 60's in her "To Sir With Love?"

About those artists I mentioned earlier, namely James Taylor, the Beach Boys, the Carpenters, the Freshmens, the Righteous Brothers and . . . . I'd like to dwell briefly on these artists, if only to divest those of you out there of the notion that my indifference toward the "The King" and the Beatles was based purely on race, rather than culture—not that I feel I have to, mind you.

Mr. James Taylor—it wouldn't be until many, many years later that I would begin to associate the name (and the man) with those memorable recordings, particularly "You've Got A Friend," and "Carolina In My Mind." His music —soft, mellow and folksy—was definitely music for reflection.

On a scale of one to four, if I had to rate the Beach Boys, I would give them a five! Maybe it doesn't make sense but that gives you some idea of what I thought of them and if I had to sing their praises, it would be ad infinitum. The Beach Boys, in my opinion, epitomized the 'good times' of the sixties—sun, fun, beaches, surfing, girls, love, etc. If ever a group fitted the so-called 'All-American' image it was the Beach Boys. On the surface, you couldn't find anything wrong with their presentation—clean-cut, their dress was simple, their music (not provocative) clean and wholesome. "Don't Worry Baby" and "All Summer Long" said it all for me. The Carpenters—ah yes, the Carpenters. I remember many a summer nights sitting in my favorite seat on the sofa near the opened door, taking in the warm sultry air and listening to the crickets outside with a 'thirty-three' of the Carpenters on the phonograph. They had this soft, mellow sound that seemed to touch the soul; The same might be said for the Freshmens. The Righteous Brothers (Bill Medley and Bobby Hatfield) attracted my attention because of their ability to sing 'outside the box.' Nay, 'outside *their* box', meaning they had the ability to sing and sound other than what they essentially were—white singers. Their sound and deliverance was just so different from other artists of their type.

During my lifetime, there has been many memorable moments. Some more memorable than others—one such moment took place in the latter seventies. I was napping in my home one evening, having fallen asleep with the television on, when I was awakened by what seemed like a nudge. As I became more lucid, I heard the crooning voice of a tall, bearded singer on the Merv Griffin Show. That singer—Thedore DeReese Pendergrass—known more affectionately as Teddy Pendergrass. He had been singing for quite some time before appearing on Merv's show that evening but he had been a member of the group, Harold Melvin and the Bluenotes. Now, he had gone solo and his star was getting brighter as his new career progressed.

Let's turn now to another genre or style of music. For the setting, let's go out to the desert at the Sands. There were names like Frank Sinatra, Dean Martin, Tony Bennett and Sammy as in Sammy Davis Jr. I have purposely placed Sammy's name here at the end here because

I want to touch briefly on Sammy's effect on the 60's and the Sands. I can't recall any other performer with, *maybe,* and I emphasize 'maybe' with the exception of Frank (Sinatra) and Ella (Fitzgerald) that had more credibility with one name. Sammy had star power! His first name became synonymous with fame, money and stardom. In the entertainment circle, just dropping his name elevated a conversation to another level or lent a degree of civility to an otherwise lackluster exchange between 'wannabees', socialites and bonafide stars. You might ask how did this come to be. Well, Sammy having been in show business since the age of four, had established himself in the minds of many as a superstar among stars. He was also a rebel and proved it when he married out of his race to May Britt. Subsequently, there was talk of Sammy and the mob having it out about . . . . Years later Sammy became good friends with people like Frank Sinatra, Dean Martin, Joey Bishop and other top names in the business. Somewhere along the line all these things came together in Sammy's career to give him influence and an incomparable appeal. Before I move on, I'd like to say something about Sinatra. The singing tone and range of many artist is good when they're first starting out in their career and they're able to maintain that level of ability as time progresses for let's say a span of thirty to forty years but after that 'window' their ability becomes suspect. Frank Sinatra demonstrated the exact opposite. His singing, like fine vintage wine, just got better over the years and he was able to sing into his eighties!

CHAPTER 4

LET'S FAST FORWARD now to the early 70's. I'm in my latter years in high school and the black kids are wearing their hair long and sculpting it into what was called an *Afro*; White kids are wearing their hair far pass what is considered 'acceptable' lengths at that time. As I began to get out more and make trips to downtown Charleston, I saw, in extreme cases, young white guys wearing their hair down their backs. These types, in rare instances, wore no shoes, tie-dyed tee shirts from the 60's and, invariably, conveyed a disheveled appearance. Owing to these things, they were dubbed either as 'hippies,' 'yippies' or beatniks. I must admit though they were few in numbers and those that were seen downtown were found south of Calhoun Street in the business district along King Street.

Charleston in the early 70's was a microcosm of the nation as a whole. There were bell-bottom trousers, platform shoes, the Afros, long hair, etc. More often than not, I recall the urban black kids being the wearers of chic, trendy clothes as opposed to the more conservative, preppy clothes worn by their white counterparts. Having gone to various integrated schools, I find myself in a rather unique position—that of a person who has been exposed to both black and white dress fashions.

Since whites comprised a majority of the students at the schools I attended, I'll dwell on white dress fashions in the latter 60's and early 70's first. Charleston County was and still is, I would imagine, heavily Jewish. I say Charleston County and not Charleston, per se, because virtually all the Jewish communities were in the surrounding areas of Charleston but they did send their kids to various schools in Charleston proper. The 'white kids', as I called them, in my classes had names like Goldberg, Bluestein, Engels, Lowenstein, etc. These kids were the offshoots of those neighboring Jewish communities and, additionally, the sons and daughters of . . . .

I have purposely avoided completing the thought I started in the last sentence of the last paragraph. I've done so because I am about to give my assessment or perspective of white dress fashion (at my school in the 60's and 70's) which encompassed the Jewish and non-Jewish Protestants. In doing so, I will mention thought-provoking words like 'values' and 'principles' that, to some extent, influenced the dress patterns of those students. Additionally, if I were to come out and overtly say in specific terms what viewpoints I had about a particular race or religious group, someone, no doubt, will be offended. As a nation, we've come a long way in terms of political correctness. So much so, that at times we've become overly sensitive and politically correct to a fault. For this reason, I will henceforth refer to the Jewish and non-Jewish Protestants simply as 'groups'. Initially, I considered labeling the two groups as *groupA* and *group B* or *group1* and *group 2* but then, came to my senses, realizing all too soon that people might misconstrue my intent—to provide a plausible means of discussing both groups without inciting prejudice and envy. Labeling them as I previously planned would have, no doubt, evoked an associative learned response from my readers. Who can deny that they wouldn't be tempted to consider *GroupA* over *GroupB* or *Group1* over or superior to *Group2.*

Traditionally, one group has always been a conservative people with conservative values and principles and lest I forget—a prudent people. I make the last point because having attended schools with the offsprings of these people, I was, more often than not, confounded by the practical façade, some of them conveyed at school. I use the term 'confounded' because I knew these kids had fathers and uncles that owned stores in downtown Charleston and these stores were pulling in easily at least six figures a year and yet when the kids came to school, one would never know! Now, getting back to the dress fashions—there were two types of dress among my fellow white students. One group—having a conservative upbringing—were more prone to a simple dress code which consisted of 'penny' loafers, tasseled shoes, khaki trousers / skirts, and shirts /blouses with matching socks. The other group were more apt to dress with the times, so to speak. They wore flair bottom jeans, hip-huggers, western-style boots, moccasins, etc. Their hair styles differed from that of their counterpart in that in most instances, it was much longer and . . . . I guess it would be a fair assumption to say that the values that this kind espoused were akin to the values that gave birth to the revolutionary counterculture of the sixties. There was also a matter of a group having access to more monies and thereby having the luxury of affording a better lifestyle. Having access to more money enabled a female, for example, in one of the groups to visit a hairstylist every week to maintain that prim and proper image that was so symbolic of the 60's. Sometimes it was not a matter of money but more a matter of values. A male of a particular group, for example, who had been reared amongst conservative values might have visited the barber every two or three weeks to keep the length of his hair at what he was told was an 'acceptable' and 'decent' length. Male members of the other group, reared in more liberal terms, may have worn their hair at an extended length to make a social and/or political statement. I'll let my readers figure out which group was which or which group adhered to the values just mentioned but I think I've already given it away.

Negroes, as they were called in the 60's, were witnessing an evolution, so to speak. They were becoming more and more political or Marxist in their views; Additionally, they were discovering racial pride, thanks to people like James Brown, Angela Davis, Macolm X, the Black Panthers and Stokely Carmichael. All this translated into fashions and trends indicative of the political atmosphere. There were dashikis, Afros and full-length leather coats worn OUTSIDE my school. Inside the school and my classes, the blacks dressed rather conservatively overall. There didn't seem to be any need to make political statements in the way of dress barring the Afro, a hairstyle very popular among young black Americans at that time. Another popular trend among both black and white Americans was the wearing of Converse All-Star sneakers. Blacks more so. No self-respecting young black male's ensemble was complete without a pair of Converse.

Coming up in the schools of Charleston, I remember always dressing well or being fashion-conscious. Although we did not have money, per se,

my mother, somehow, always afforded me decent shoes and clothing—
something I think contributed immensely to my self-imagery and
self-esteem. In my latter years in high school, when my mother could
no longer afford to buy me clothes, I got various jobs downtown and
continued to dress well. At the height of my sartorial indulgence, a typical
ensemble might have included a burgundy, polka-dot shirt having a
white collar and French cuffs with contrasting tan, flaired-bottom slacks
that fell on brown shoes in such a fashion as to expose only the toe tips
of the shoes.

I had derived my fashion and style-savvy early on from two people
in my community while living on Elizabeth Street in Charleston: (1) a
Baptist minister and (2) an upstairs neighbor. The minister, who lived
two doors down, pastored the church on the corner adjacent to his house.
In retrospect, I would have to say that he was the quintessential Baptist
minister, as it were. Yes, he *was* black. Yes, he *did* drive a Cadillac and
yes, he was charismatic. Imagine, if you will, a black Caesar Romero only
with more finesse, if such a thing is possible. Tall, immaculately-groomed
right down to his nails with an easy-going manner. He and his wife who
could have doubled for Zora Neale Hurston could very easily have been
nominated poster couple by some exclusive, fashionable magazine for
handsomest couple. The other person—my upstairs neighbor—lived with
his grandmother on the second floor. All week long I'd see him come
home from work in nondescript clothes that gave him the appearance
of blending into the scenery but on Friday evenings, he'd come home,
as usual, and spend 2-3 hours upstairs transforming himself. When he'd
come downstairs to go out for the evening, he would be dressed in typical
fashion for the times in perhaps a white suit, white pointed-toe shoes
with a cool blue pastel shirt and contrasting white tie. Where before he

had always worn a stocking cap, his head would now be bare revealing a close crop of wavy hair, combed and brushed to meticulous perfection and as he'd walk off into the evening, there was always the lingering smell of pungent cologne.

CHAPTER 5

BETWEEN '68 AND '72 my mother, brothers, sister and I lived on a project development or as some would say, 'da pro-jeks' on Jackson Street. My fondest memories of life on Jackson Street were perhaps waking up Saturday mornings to the Rascals, "A Beautiful Morning," or Chicago's "Saturday In The Park" or even the sound of my 'first love' yelling out from her house to her neighbor and best friend a few doors down from us. My 'first love,' as I called her, was the first girl to make an impression on me. Whenever I saw her, I felt . . . . And I wanted so much to talk to her and be in the company of her but I could never bring myself to do it. Physically, she was striking—big-boned, black as the blackest night with the dreamiest eyes. To this very day I don't thing she knew how I felt about her.

The immediate community was proverbially 'tight-knit' with everybody knowing everybody. The atmosphere during this time was such that you could leave your door open when visiting neighbors or . . . . I recall vividly on many occasions, having walked into neighbors' homes, looking for my mother and finding the door(s) open and the homes unattended.

About this time in my experience, I was rapidly reaching puberty and so were the other kids of my peer group in the complex. About two doors down from us were the Singletons—father, mother and six kids. Two of the kids (girls) were slightly older than I. They were heralding new styles in women's clothing and accessories, specifically mini-dresses, 'fishnet' and 'window pane' stockings. The mini-dress which had been made popular by a young lady out of London by the name of Lesley Hornby (Twiggy) was worn by all the pubescent young ladies hoping to catch the eyes of potential suitors. The 'window pane' and 'fishnet' stockings were radical-looking and like the mini-dress, very eye-catching. Funny thing about these stockings—its sex appeal seemed to increase twofold when they became tattered, consequently attracting the baser instincts in the opposite sex. So much so that for over a decade or more in various settings across the country after there introduction, coquettes and streetwalkers would intentionally wear them (in tattered condition) to attract the attention of men.

About this same time, the 'big boys' (older boys) were making the local merchants and haberdasheries, in downtown Charleston, rich. They were wearing bright, outlandish-colored silk pants— green, pink, orange, blue.etc. with Italian imported shoes, shirts and hats—all of which were worn in various matching color schemes. A multi-patterned shirt, for example, with multiple colors would be matched with a colored trouser matching one of the colors in the shirt. To round out the statement, the boys would wear shoes and hats to match the trouser.

Now, I'm not certain whether this was a pervasive style across America or a regional 'thing', as they say, but what I am certain about are the shoes, called platform shoes. They were definitely the rage across America. I bought my first pair in 1972.

In about the early part of '71 the nation and indeed the world witnessed a spectacular sporting event between a South Carolinian named Joe Frazier and Cassius Clay who was now going by the name of Muhamad Ali. I recall days later after the fight reading in various papers and magazines of the resplendent style and dress of the people that attended the fight arena at Madison Square Garden that night. There were full length minks, ermines, and dazzling, eye-blinding jewelry. So ostentatious and memorable was the fashion statements that night that it has become synonymous—in my mind—with the historic fight itself.

The morning after the fight in my homeroom class, there was much talk of the fight. This fight was of particular importance to the people of South Carolina because Joe Frazier hailed from the palmetto state. Even so though, I would say that a very large percentage of the young people of South Carolina were rooting for Muhammad Ali at that time; This is how popular Ali was. If I remember correctly, Ali was knocked down in the 15th round of the fight by the smaller Joe Frazier. To understand the strength and power behind a punch that decked a full-grown, 6' 2" man of 230 lbs., let's take a look at one of South Carolina's most famous sons, Joe Frazier. For those of you who are not up to date on your history, you'd be well-advised to know that South Carolina was the entry port for prime stock slaves. It was here that the strongest slaves who had managed to weather the long and arduous ship ride from Africa to America, first found themselves. It was here that these same slaves who were undoubtedly the strongest of those shipped, worked and toiled in fields for long hours, harvesting rice and performing Herculean tasks that no other human would or could do. Now, couple what I've just told you with the fact that South Carolina has always had a rich agronomy and farming industry. Additionally, South Carolina—Charleston particularly— is right on the coast where seafood is plentiful. Having grown up in South Carolina and ultimately visiting other parts of the country, I've been able to make a distinction in the foods. I found the food in South Carolina to be richer and better-tasting—the milk creamier, the egg yolks yellowier and then there's that staple, grits. As for seafood, I don't think, and I may be biased in saying so having lived in South Carolina, but I don't think there is any better-tasting seafood in the whole country than that of the palmetto state.

Getting back to Joe Frazier, I strongly suspect that Joe is a direct descendant of those first slaves with no blood depletion in his lineage. What does this mean? This means that he inherited the full strength of his forefathers sans racial intermingling that could possibly have weakened or depleted his genetic make-up and may I add that growing up in South Carolina with access to all that rich food couldn't help but fortify those natural strengths. So we know that Joe had two things going for him—his lineage and his having had access to all that rich food that is so prevalent in South Carolina. I read a biographical account of Joe Frazier's life story once and it said that Joe left home (South Carolina) at the age of fifteen. If this is true—and I have every reason to believe that it is—non-residents and out-of-staters might question the second premise of my theory—that Joe Frazier's strength was partly due to the rich food in South Carolina, on the grounds that food could not have been that big a factor since Joe left home so early in his life. But I beg to differ; I've witnessed firsthand what a steady diet of fresh, rich food products only hours away from the nearest farm can do to pubescence in a state such as South Carolina. Young boys of fifteen or so appear to be bigger, if not stronger, than fully grown men and a young girl of twelve or thirteen, coming into puberty before boys, have the appearance of fully grown women. Resorting to a little southern colloquialism, I'd say "Oh yes, They grow 'em big down thar!" Thirdly and lastly, I believe that Ali's fate was sealed with the training Joe's seasoned trainer, Yank Durham, put him through for the *Fight of the Century* as it was called.

CHAPTER 6

NOW BABY BOOMERS, do you remember the first text books you were given in grade school? Do you remember the distinct smell of those big, fat crayons they gave you? I use the term, 'distinct', to describe the smell because a first grader at the tender age of 6 finds every new smell, 'distinct', as everything at such a young age has shock value or impression on a young mind which is why even at this merry ole age of 53, I can still summon the smell in my memory bank.

Now let's get back to the text books. My text books were written by people with the names—McGraw and Hill. The names were separated by a hyphen which appeared like this, McGraw-Hill. My classmates and I were introduced to 'textbook friends' (kiddie parlance for characters) called Tom, Dick, Jerry, Alice and Jip (dog). Initially, in the textbooks we were introduced to a 'friend' with a picture of that new friend and the words, "See Jerry" or "See Alice." Subsequently, the book would have them performing some action such as running. Under them would be the words, "See Jerry run" or "See Alice run." Well, so much for that. In high school, do you recall the books that were required reading? For me, there was *The Adventures of Huckleberry Finn, The Old Man and the Sea, Catcher in the Rye, Great Expectations,* etc. I could go on but those were just a few of the books or stories the high schoolers during that time had to read.

As I stated earlier, we all have idols during our teen years. My idols were people like Angela Davis, Sly of Sly and the Family Stones fame and Elridge Cleaver. I can just see those people, of let's say, a less than liberal bent, closing their books certain that they have pigeon-holed me but may I remind the remaining objective readers that this book is not about me—the man—but rather his perception of a past era growing up in one of the country's most historic southern towns.

During the drafting of this book back on June 12, 2003 I was listening to one of my favorite talk show hosts on the radio when he announced that he would be having an author on his show talking about his new book relative to how America has changed since 1950. It struck a nerve in me because after all I had been writing—not about how things have changed since 1950—but rather about fads, styles and life in general in a small USA town. I listened to the author and subsequent callers-in (commenting) and was relieved to learn that the author sought to explain how much things have changed since 1950 as opposed to my pending book—simply conveying one man's perception of that time period as it related to his hometown. As I continued to listen to the author, he pointed out, what he thought were several key events in his book that were responsible for revolutionizing America since 1950. After making several commentaries, he and the host entertained callers who in turn gave their opinions and comments on the book and the topic itself. One caller, in particular, cited the removal of the then-Governor George Wallace from the doors of the University of Alabama in 1963 and the subsequent integration of public schools around the country as reason for what he saw as the downfall of American education. I listened attentively and thought about what had been said and then that small inner voice that had spoken to me on so many occasions and had given me clarity of vision said, "Suppose schools in America had remained segregated as it were in the 1950s with superior academic resources being offered to only a segment of the country. Wouldn't that promote a permanent upper class and underclass here in America and wouldn't we be depriving ourselves and indeed the world of possibly another Einstein?"

On or about the day I heard the author speak about his book, I learned that Mr. Gregory Peck and Mr. David Brinkley had passed away. Ironically, I had planned on mentioning David Brinkley here in my book as he was very much a part of my life in the 60s and early 70s. You see, for me, as odd as it may sound, he was part of my quiet time. Chet Huntley and he came on with the news at six-thirty every evening at a time when my mother would be in the kitchen preparing the evening's dinner. They came on at a time during the summer months when the sun would still be high in the sky but the day would be cooling off and I would be in my favorite seat on the sofa near the door taking in the summer breeze. During the winter evenings, they came on at a time when it would be dark, the house warm and comfortable from the big heater, and Moma in the kitchen. Every so often the sound of the television would be interrupted by a neighbor visiting to borrow something or just to make small talk. I can hear the two newsmen to this very day: "Good evening, I'm Chet Huntley—and I'm David Brinkley and today along the Demilitarized Zone . . . ."

CHAPTER 7

HEY, BABYBOOMERS, I'M going to guess and say that you've been through about fifteen U.S. Presidents of which you probably only saw thirteen in office. I've been through fourteen and remember seeing only twelve in office. Now, who was your most favorite President? Who was your least favorite? Now that I've got you thinking, I would like to give my opinions of those Presidents I've lived through. Of the last nine Presidents, I would have to say that President John F. Kennedy was the most charismatic. My memory of Kennedy is rather vague but I do recall he and Jacqueline as being the epitome of charm and refinement. At this point in my manuscript, I am putting in an insertion or update. Most of this writing was done five or more years ago, well before the Obamas took office. President Barack Obama is charismatic but I'm still giving the egde to former President John F. Kennedy. If I had to vote on which couple most personifies charm and refinement—the Obamas or the Kennedys —the choice would be very difficult. "Why is that?" you might ask. Individually, I have already given the edge to former President John F. Kennedy over our current President, President Barack Obama. The final decision would have to lie with the wives of the two men. Jacqueline Kennedy was a fashionista; so is Mrs. Michelle Obama. Jacqueline Kennedy, besides having been the President's wife, having lineage and having moved in the circles of the rich and powerful *looked* the part and *didn't she know it.* Currently, I saw a photo of the Obamas, a year ago, entering a state dinner and thought, if there were a Red Sea before them, it would have parted. First Lady Michelle Obama also gets very high marks for not only being a trendsetter but a symbol of humaneness and compassion. Frankly, both the current President and his wife have been symbols of kindness and compassion which has been a good thing for the country's moral perspective. I'm *not* going to make a decision at this point. To do so, I think, would be self-serving and having very little relevance.

Who was my most favorite President? Least favorite? I've never had a 'most favorite' or a 'least favorite' President, per se; However, I do have candidates (Presidents) in mind for 'most respected' and 'least respected' positions in my chronicles. As I iterated early on, I want this to be an enjoyable read for everyone, so I will not talk about the Presidents I had the least regard for as I am a firm believer in the old saw, "If you can't say something good about someone, don't say anything at all." Now, are you ready for the #1 most respected President in my chronicles? Excuse me for a moment while I get them to sound the trumpets. The President that I had the most respect for was . . . . our 38th President, Gerald R. Ford. Why Ford? I chose former President Ford for two reasons: Reason #1, prior to Ford's Presidency, no other President — would you believe—had seen fit to even thank Jesse Owens, the famed 1936 Olympian, for his memorable performance in Berlin of that year. Ford conveyed considerable substance in 1976 when he bestowed upon Jesse Owens the Presidential Medal of Freedom. Reason#2, Ford, during his Presidency, was known in and around Washington as someone who, shall we say, was less than agile on his feet but, paradoxically, I once saw him perform one of the most unbelievable acrobatic feats I had ever seen. There he was(on television) disembarking from a plane with a dignitary at the bottom of the ramp waiting to greet him. As he stepped out of the plane onto the ramp and on the first step, he went into his routine—falling and bumbling down the ramp. As he neared the bottom of the stairs, he somehow, miraculously, not only managed to upright himself but extend his hand to the waiting dignitary in a remarkable show of reverence and protocol. I said to myself, "How did he **DO-O** that?" Needless to say, I was impressed!

God only knows how many foreign leaders and splinter groups were dissuaded from doing something rash during the Presidency of our 40th President, Ronald Wilson Reagan. He, I would have to say, was our most intimidating President in the last half-century, what with the jet-black hair, dark suits and exceptional built. Did you notice the way Reagan filled out his suits? Of course you did. And If I'm not mistaken, he was seventy when he took office. Every man should look so good, if they're fortunate enough to live so long.

I think the country was most relaxed in the late seventies and into the eighties under former President Jimmy Carter, due in part to his easy-going, laid-back style and the . . . . Theoretically, I believe that a people's perception of a President or leader will ultimately cause an ascending or a descending to the level of that leader whether that perception is real or imagined as the leader (central figure) tends to have a subliminal effect on the minds of the people. I guess you could say the effect is akin to a state of mass hypnosis over the people he governs which explains why haute couture became so pervasive under John F. Kennedy or why the nation became kinder and gentler under the Carter administration. John F. Kennedy, a handsome trim figure himself, married Jacqueline Bouvier, who along with her sister, Lee Radziwill comprised one of the foremost fashion connoisseurs during this period. To further illustrate my point, have you noticed how 'touchy-feely' the nation has become ever since the Obamas came into the Presidency? The President, himself, likes to greet people with a short shake and a pat on the (upper) back; the First lady likes to greet with a warm hug. Both greetings defy past protocol but are seen as less formal and more affectionate greetings. Consequently, the whole nation seems to be hugging and slapping the back affectionately when greeting.

Of course, there are exceptions to every rule and the Nixon Administration was just such an exception. I believe it was Abraham Lincoln that said, "You can fool some of the people some of the time but you can't fool all of the people all of the time." Case in point, former President Richard Nixon's Administration—a symbol of conservatism—was one that espoused conservative views and laws but for some reason, a whole counterculture of social peripherals—'hippies', 'yippies' and 'beatniks'—were spawned under his Presidency.

By the way, I think we should give some recognition to former President Jimmy Carter for having introduced America to a 'kinder and gentler' concept who even after leaving office, continued to perpetuate the idea, by working with Habitat and building homes for the socially-disadvantaged. I might add here also that John F. Kennedy was also up for nomination as the most 'kinder and gentler' President but Mr. Carter won hands down as there was just a number of things in his mannerism or character that led me to choose him for having introduced America to the concept of kindness and compassion. Under the Reagan administration, did you notice that we became more intense? Also, there was the matter of the 'r' word being mentioned more than in the previous two administrations. Was this all attributed to Mr. Reagan or the perception of Mr. Reagan? Before I delve into my opinions, thoughts and comments regarding our fortieth President who I believe was one of our more interesting, if not the most interesting, President in the last fifty years, let's hark back to the saw I made reference to in describing my feelings about talking about someone—"If you can't say something nice about someone, don't say anything at all (about that person)." So, in forging ahead, let me assure those of you out there who may think that I will say something improper and/or disrespectful about our deceased former President—that I will not. On the contrary, I'm of the opinion that Ronald Reagan (and Nancy) were decent and honorable Americans. I've included the former First Lady here because she is a big fan of one of my favorite singers, Johnny Mathis, and anyone who likes the music of Johnny Mathis has got to be an exceptionally tasteful person. Getting back to our former President, I would say that his Presidency was based more on imagery and perception than substance. Abroad, he was viewed as a 'two-gun totin' cowboy' whose hands were always just a few inches away from the holster. This image translated into an obdurate war hawk, of sorts. Here at home, he was being viewed dichotomously as both a decent and respectable President by some and a not so decent President by others who thought he was either of that ilk who believed in what amounted to the 'r' word or at the very least, his Presidency helped to foster an atmosphere which alienated various ethnicities.

Let's see now, what in Mr. Reagan's image had managed to stir up such visceral feelings abroad and at home? Well, early on in his career he had come to personify the very essence of conservatism. Additionally, he became a Republican—two factors that his opponents would use to misconstrue the ideology and political views behind the politician with the essence of the man. About the physical stats of the man—he was over 6 feet with dark black hair which tended to give him a menacing look of sorts.

Before I go on, I find it necessary to reiterate that I personally believe that Mr. Reagan was a good and decent man—at heart— but his image, unfortunately, was not a palatable one for a man of his complexion. He moved too confidently and then there was that ever-present swagger. As most of us know, Mr. Reagan succeeded Mr. Jimmy Carter in office and because the two men had completely different styles, ideologies and party affiliations, the back—to-back Administrations offered a stark contrast.

Mr. Jimmy Carter, an easy-going, soft-spoken, 'How-ya'll-doin'-Mister Rodgers-type liberal from Georgia was turning over the Office to Ronald Wilson Reagan, a dyed-in the-wool conservative who appeared to be a John Wayne clone and an archetype for such men as the NRA advocate to come later—Charlton 'from-my-cold-dead-hands' Heston.

So here we had Mr. Reagan, an arch conservative whose reputation had preceded him, taking office. If ever there was a case of mass hypnosis—this was it. A very large segment of America had so misperceived our incoming President. Some doing so out of naiivete, others out of some inherent necessity to fulfill, perhaps, an idealistic need. This 'segment' of which I speak consisted of the rich and the poor, the naiive and the supposedly 'intelligent,' and finally people of all hues. To illustrate my point I could cite an embarrassing incident that occurred among the arrangers of the Inaugural Ball for Mr. Reagan who I am almost certain had no prior knowledge of that evening's festivities but to do so, would take us into the abyss and I'm not willing to go there.

I never gave much thought to the man, Richard Milhous Nixon per se, but I confess I was a bit disturbed by his burial ceremony in the garden of the White House. Mr. Nixon, during his Presidency, had done some less than honorable things, to say the least. Now, the former President of the United States of America was dead and the people in charge of arranging his burial were put in a very awkward situation. They couldn't very well adhere to the standard protocol held for past Presidents. To do so, would have sent mixed messages to Americans and the world-at-large.

I want to talk now about an icon whose solvency is still strong as ever but whose image (at least in my mind) has taken a beating over the years—the bank. The bank?? Yes, the bank! Banks have always been around for as long as communities of people. They were builted specifically to accommodate the financial needs and aspirations of the community. Growing up in the 60s and 70s, a bank might have been compared to a god, if I may so. I say this because a bank's beginnings was unknown and it would be expected to exist into eternity; it was revered as a a monolithic icon of the establishment. So secure were they in their future that their names were carved in stone on the frontages and it was believed by some that the banks were the actual owners of the buildings they occupied.

Sometime in the 80s, smaller banks or banks with less assets were taken over by larger banks. Names changed, some became insolvent and were even seen closing their doors. The whole image of banking was taking a battering. When they did open or announce a name change, they did so with paper banners, subsequently replaced with metal signs. Gone were the images of banks of olden days—at least in my mind—with carved-in-stone frontages and Romanesque architecture.

Things have changed greatly in the last fifty years and for me just to make such a statement is or might be considered a no-brainer or as my daughter would say, "Duh-h!" The progression of time—a fact of life—has brought with it the progression of technology and other changes, some good—some not so good. I was in New York City a few years ago and saw a hooded young man with his hands in his pockets, his head lowered and walking toward me on the sidewalk. He appeared to be mumbling to himself. As he walked pass me, I saw what looked like a long cylindrical tube (microphone) in front of his mouth. Inwardly, I started laughing because here I was, a babyboomer who had witnessed the proliferation of landline phones, then cell phones and now here was a 'hands-free' telephone. My first impression, I must admit, was that here approaching me was one of those deranged people on the skids.

Fifty years ago, television viewers were more apt to fall asleep with the television on only to wake up subsequently to a deafening sound of a signed-off station. Today, television viewers have the remote with which they can turn their sets off when they feel themselves falling asleep or they can program their set to turn off automatically after a predetermined time. Fifty years ago, it was considered a badge of honor in the eyes of neighbors and peers for a parent to reprimand (physically) a child for what was viewed as a punishable offense; Today, a parent, beating his or her child, is more likely to be given a scarlet letter if not thrown into jail. I was dining out recently and finishing my meal, I motioned to the server, as they are now called, with a writing gesture, indicating that I was ready for the bill. I got an odd stare and then I think it dawned on her that I was asking for the check. That stare was more than likely due to the fact that they don't give written checks to customers any more—they're computer generated.

Fifty years ago, I was a big lover of chocolate milk and to this very day, I still am. In the early sixties, milk was delivered to many homes across the U.S. by milkmen and our family was one of them. Charleston was surrounded by a number of dairy farms and the close proximity, I guess, accounted for the good fresh taste of the milk. For days after the milkman had delivered bottled quarts of white and chocolate milk, I found myself sneaking into the refrigerator and drinking the chocolate milk out of the bottle. My mother, being upstairs when this was happening would hear the refrigerator open and sensing something was up would say, "Rudolph, what are you doin' in the refrigerator?" I'd say, "Nuttin' mom." Do you suppose my mom knew what I was doing? Of course she did. Mothers are some of the keenest people in the world when it comes to their kids. Getting back to the chocolate milk, fifty years ago it was creamier with just the right consistency. Today, the government has stepped in and has started regulating the making of chocolate milk—having come to the conclusion that chocolate milk in its purest state is to rich and contributes to obesity. Whenever I go to the stores today looking for chocolate milk, I always inevitably and indubitably find chocolate milk with the labels, 'lowfat,' 'fat-free,' and/or 'reduced fat.' No-o, things just ain't [sic] the way they useta [sic] be.

Well folks, I feel myself grasping for straws here but I must say it's been fun and I can only hope it's been the same for you. To you my readers, particularly my fellow babyboomers, I wish you love and may you live another fifty years. May God be with you!

Finis

ABOUT THE AUTHOR

RUDOLPH F. WIGGINS, formerly Rudolph Frazier hails from Charleston, South Carolina and atternded public grade schools, a high school and one college preparatory school (Charleston High) there. Mr. Wiggins is a freelance writer and an occasional context writer with two online websites—fuszball.com and fuszball.com/blog. One of Mr. Wiggins' claim to fame there in Charleston was that he met with Elizabeth O'Neil Verner in the 70's, a chance meeting which ultimately enabled him to indulge in his chosen passion at that time—art. Like most residents of Charleston, South Carolina, Mr. Wiggins experienced all the charm and gentility of one of the south's most beloved cities and one of the county's most historic.